SONG BOOK NO

This Song Book Belongs

Eleanor Elizabeth Gore-Rowe

SONGWRITER INFORMATION

PHONE NUMBER: _____ EMAIL ADDRESS: _____

ADDRESS: _____

CITY: _____ STATE: _____ ZIP: _____

NOTES

ARTIST NAME: _____ WEBSITE: _____

Copyright © 2021 Songwriter's Journal & Notebook: Songwriting Lyric, Hook, Title and Rhyme Ideas with Guitar Chords, Tablature and Staff Paper for Songwriting Manuscript Compositions

All rights reserved. No part of this book may be reproduced in any form or by any electronic or mechanical means, including information storage and retrieval systems, without permission in writing from the publisher, except by reviewers, who may quote brief passages in a review.

Professional Musicians Publishing

MY SONG COLLECTION
- TABLE OF CONTENTS -

SONG TITLE	#
☆ Rap about how awfull my parents are! ☆	1
	2
	3
	4
	5
	6
	7
	8
	9
	10
	11
	12
	13
	14
	15
	16
	17
	18
	19
	20
	21
	22
	23
	24
	25

1 SONG Title: My PARENTS!!!

Date Started: Date Completed:

SONG BRAINSTORMING NOTES (Jot down ideas for the song)

Song Set-Up & Chords

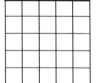 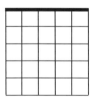 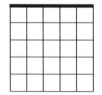

TUNING: **CAPO:**   **KEY:**

STRUM PATTERN:

PICK PATTERN:

Song Lyrics

This is a story all about how my parents just dork all about, and how they use their mushy minds to take away my all divine.
Do they <u>no how it feels</u> <u>NO</u>!! I wish they could and feel woe! They make up lie's that I despise and when I'm low, ignore my crys.

(3 second pause)

Now dont get me started on my dad, he thinks he's funny, but he's just bad, and he thinks he's great. but he's ~~really~~ just sad. But, come on, lets move on, still got mum to get ooner left or right, lose or tight. Thinks everything is fine, but when it's time to dine things cross the line.

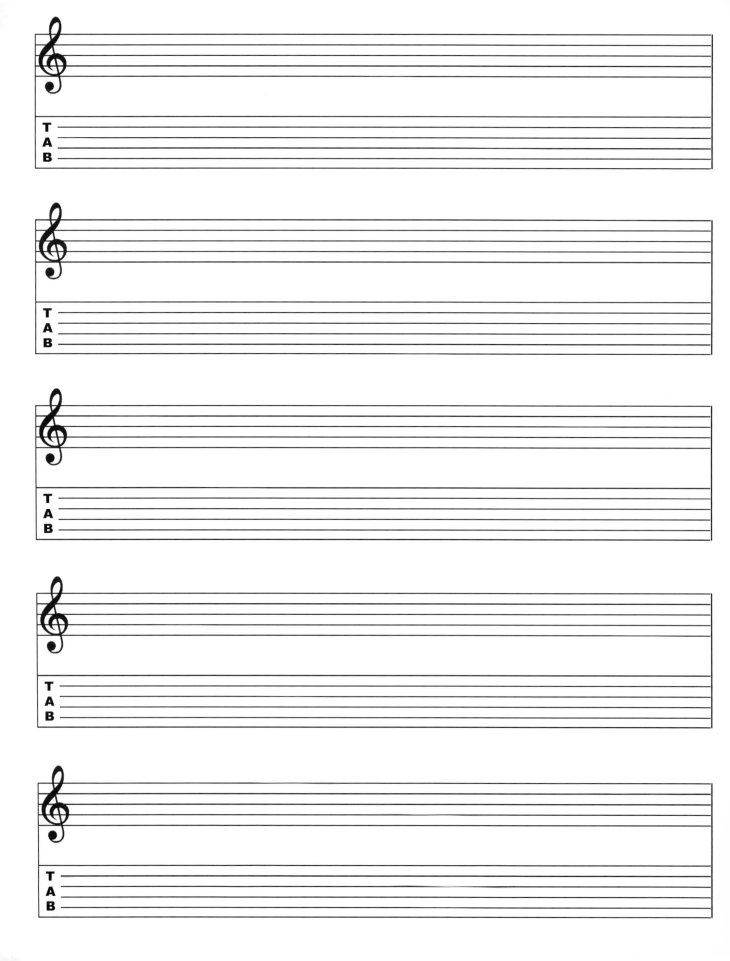

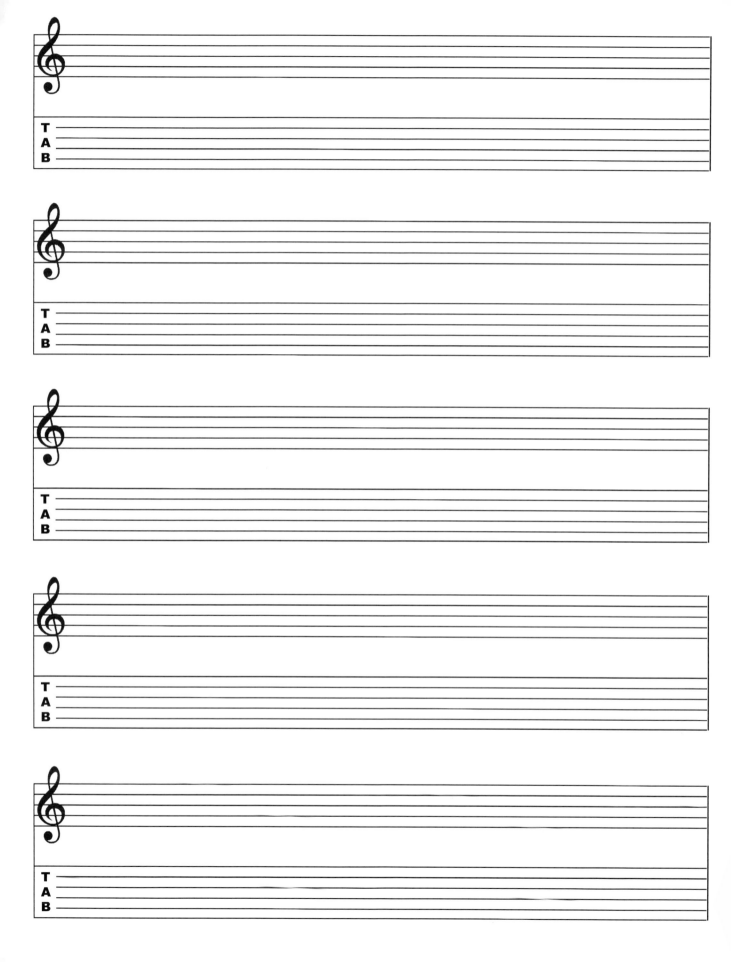

| 2 | **SONG** *Title* _____

Date Started: Date Completed:

SONG BRAINSTORMING NOTES (Jot down ideas for the song)

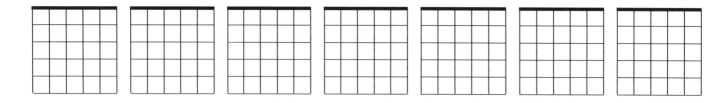

Song Set-Up & Chords

TUNING: **CAPO:**   **KEY:**

STRUM PATTERN:

PICK PATTERN:

Song Lyrics

INTRO

VERSE

CHORUS/HOOK

OUTRO

OTHER

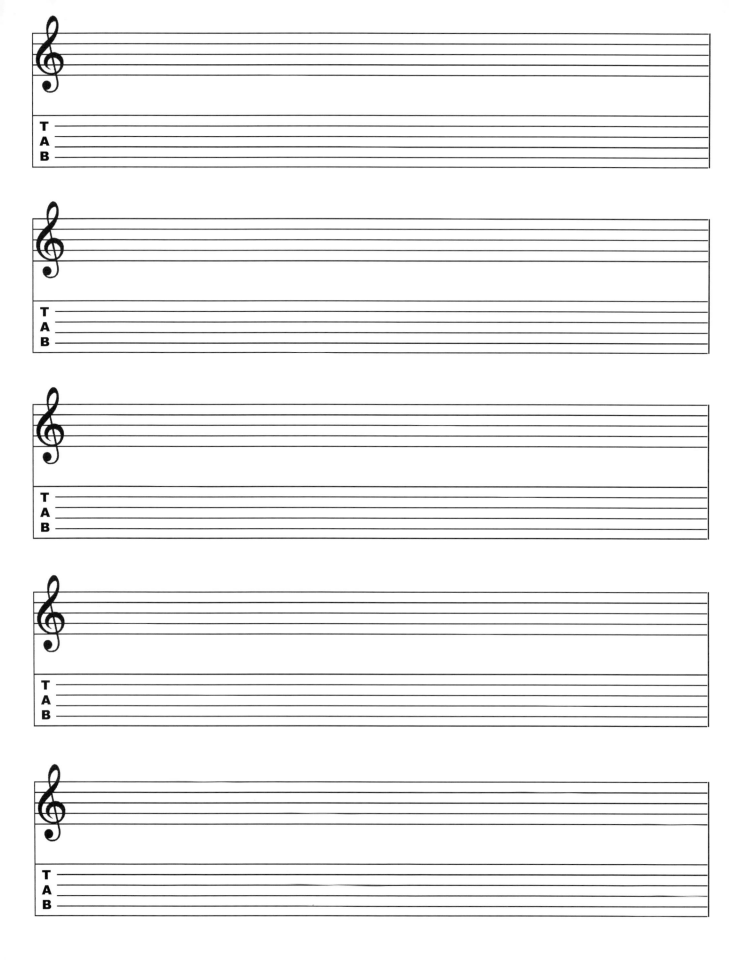

| 3 | **SONG** *Title* _____

Date Started: Date Completed:

SONG BRAINSTORMING NOTES (Jot down ideas for the song)

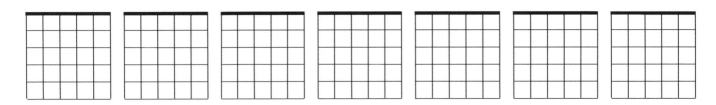

Song Set-Up & Chords

TUNING: **CAPO:**   **KEY:**

STRUM PATTERN:

PICK PATTERN:

Song Lyrics

INTRO

VERSE

CHORUS/HOOK

OUTRO

OTHER

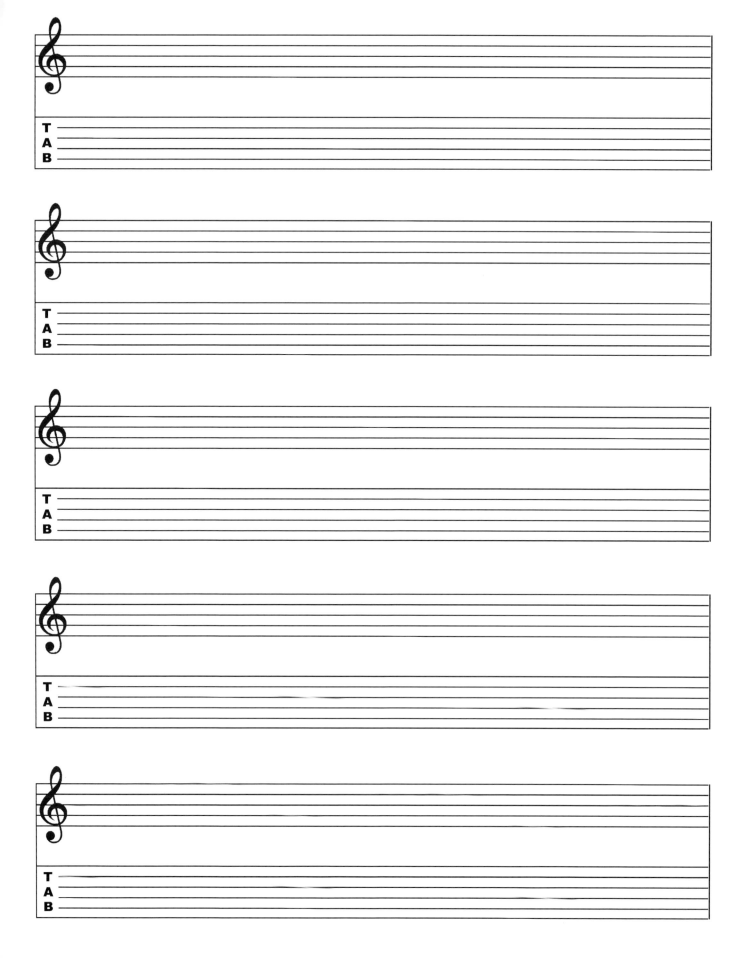

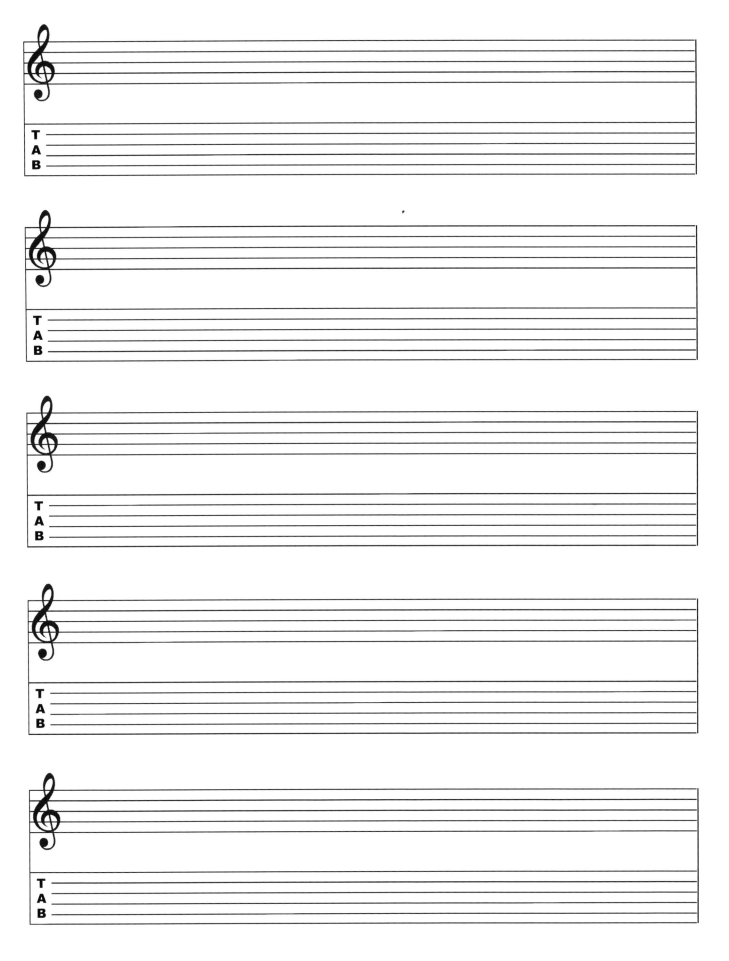

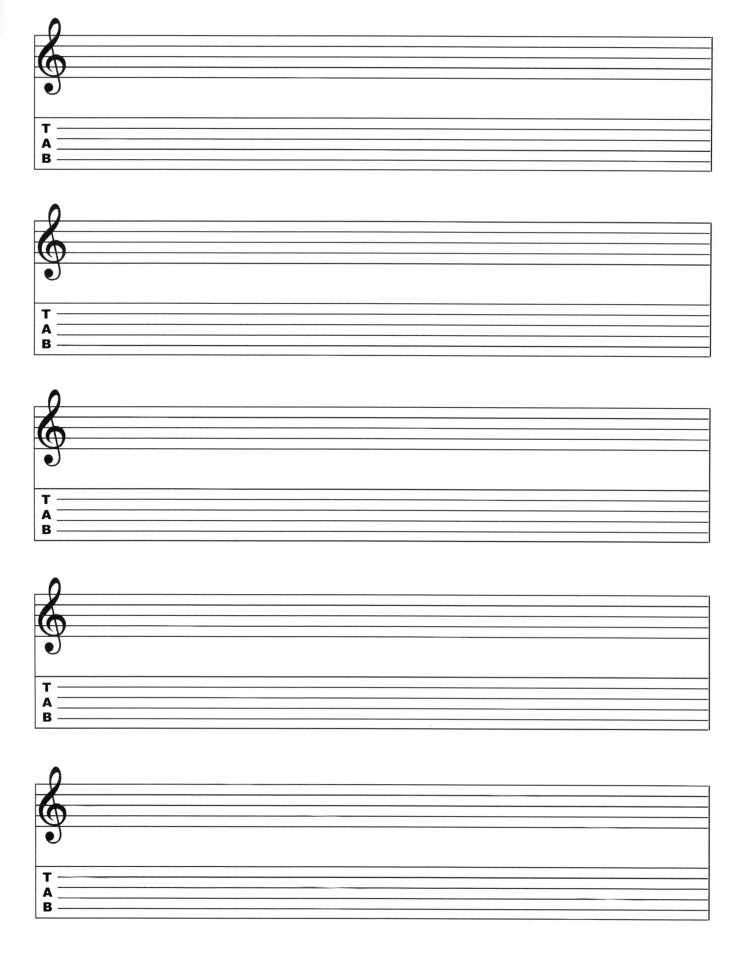

| 4 | **SONG** *Title* _____

Date Started: Date Completed:

SONG BRAINSTORMING NOTES (Jot down ideas for the song)

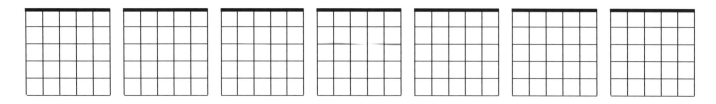

TUNING: **CAPO:**   **KEY:**

STRUM PATTERN:

PICK PATTERN:

Song Lyrics

INTRO

VERSE

CHORUS/HOOK

OUTRO

OTHER

| 5 | **SONG** *Title* _____

Date Started: _____ Date Completed: _____

SONG BRAINSTORMING NOTES (Jot down ideas for the song)

Song Set-Up & Chords

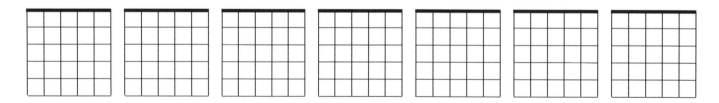

TUNING: **CAPO:**   **KEY:**

STRUM PATTERN:

PICK PATTERN:

Song Lyrics

INTRO

VERSE

CHORUS/HOOK

OUTRO

OTHER

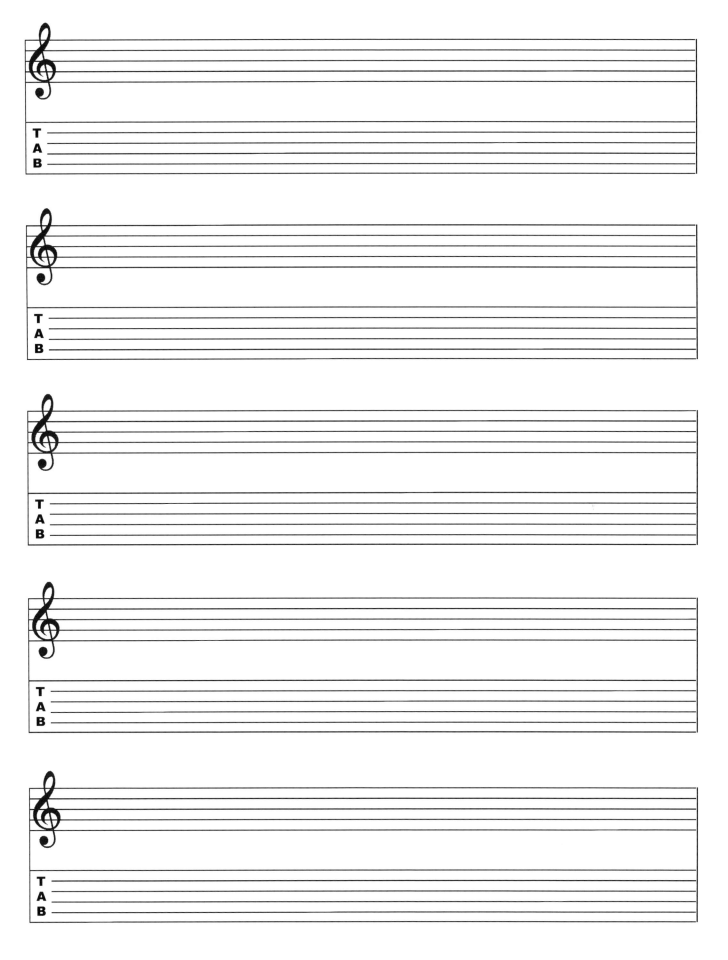

| 6 | **SONG** *Title* _____

Date Started: Date Completed:

SONG BRAINSTORMING NOTES (Jot down ideas for the song)

Song Set-Up & Chords

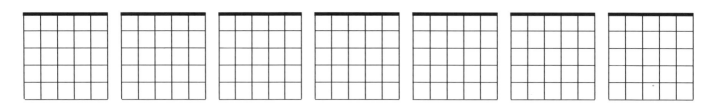

TUNING: **CAPO:**   **KEY:**

STRUM PATTERN:

PICK PATTERN:

Song Lyrics

INTRO

VERSE

CHORUS/HOOK

OUTRO

OTHER

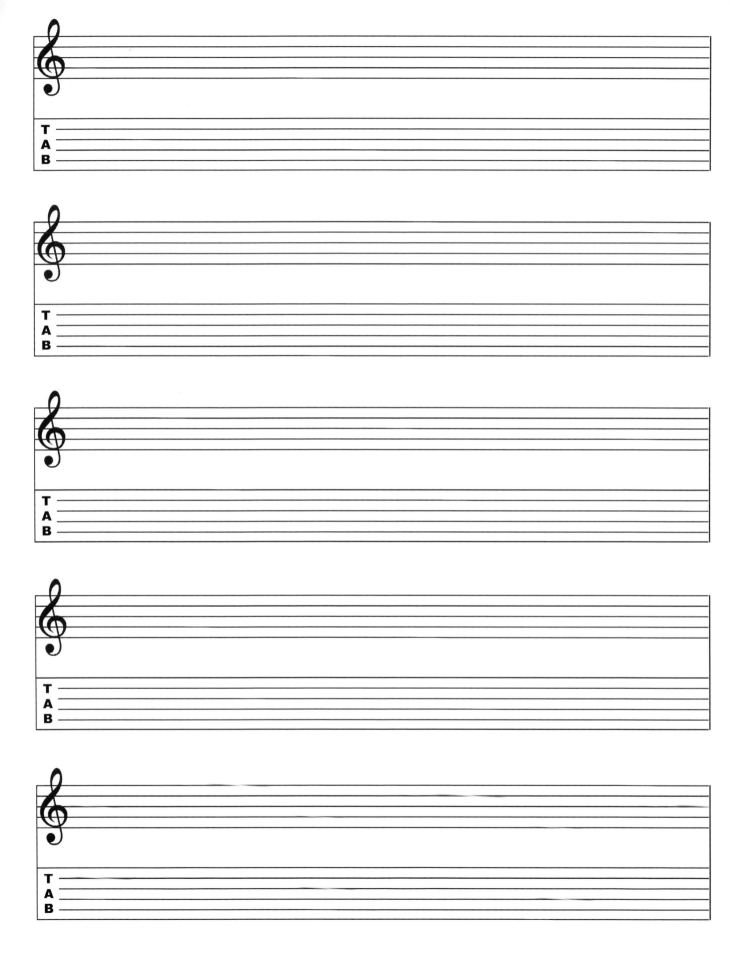

| 7 | **SONG** *Title* _____

Date Started: Date Completed:

SONG BRAINSTORMING NOTES (Jot down ideas for the song)

―――――― *Song Set-Up & Chords* ――――――

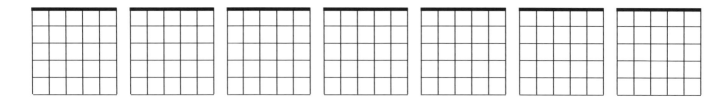

TUNING: **CAPO:**   **KEY:**

STRUM PATTERN:

PICK PATTERN:

Song Lyrics

INTRO

VERSE

CHORUS/HOOK

OUTRO

OTHER

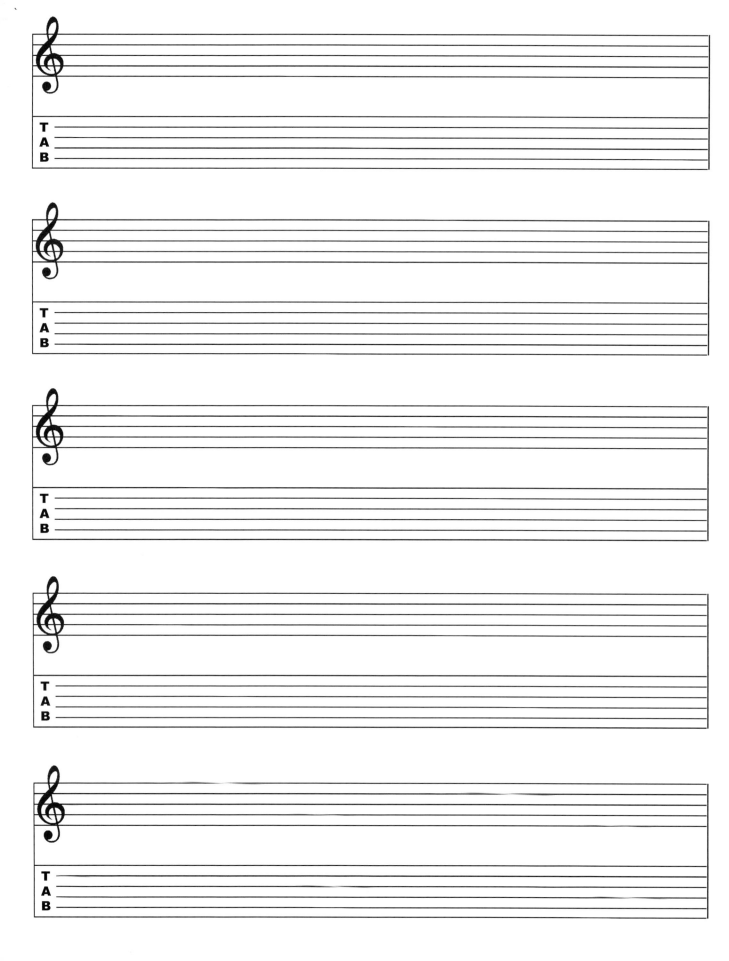

| 8 | **SONG** *Title* _____

Date Started: Date Completed:

SONG BRAINSTORMING NOTES (Jot down ideas for the song)

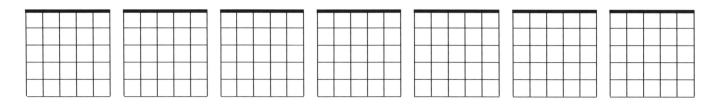

Song Set-Up & Chords

TUNING: **CAPO:**   **KEY:**

STRUM PATTERN:

PICK PATTERN:

Song Lyrics

INTRO

VERSE

CHORUS/HOOK

OUTRO

OTHER

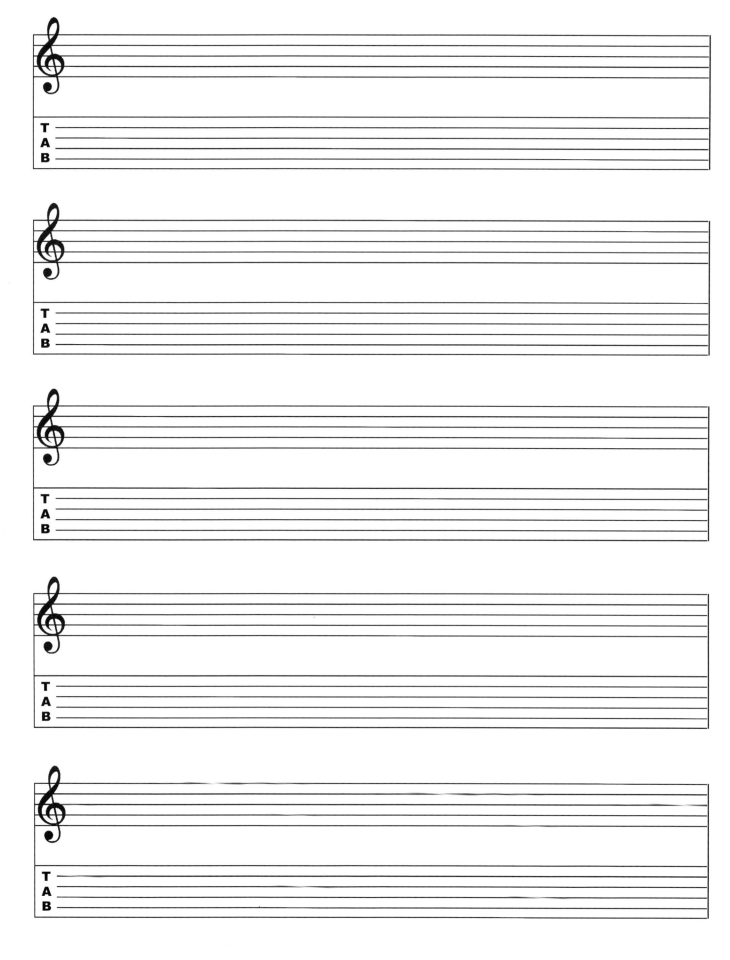

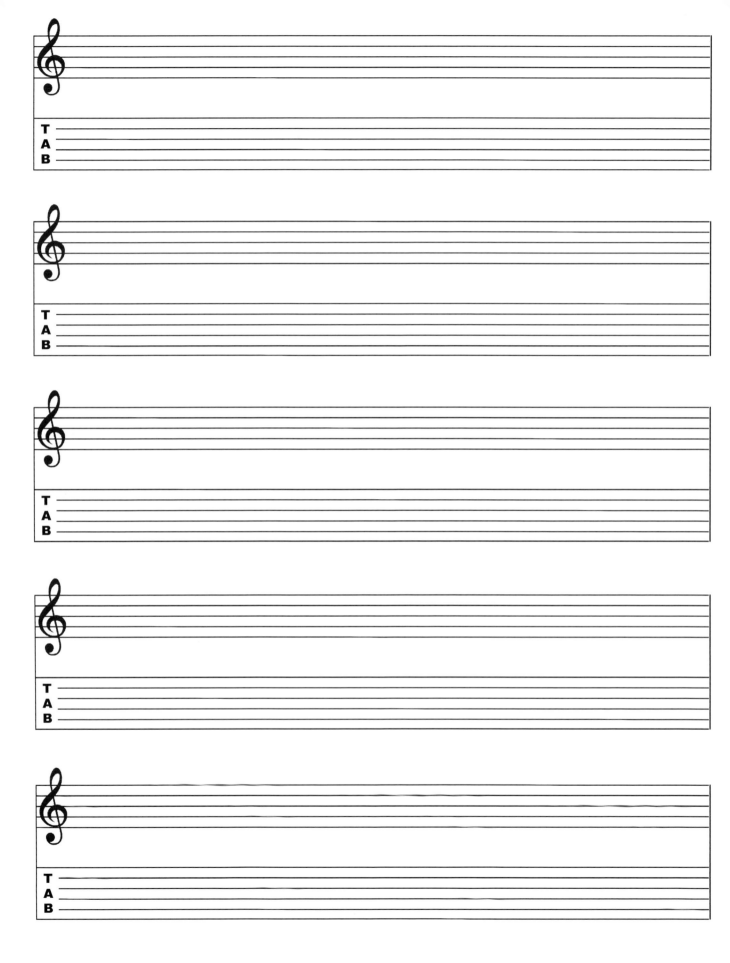

| 9 | **SONG** *Title* _____

Date Started:　　　　　　　　Date Completed:

SONG BRAINSTORMING NOTES (Jot down ideas for the song)

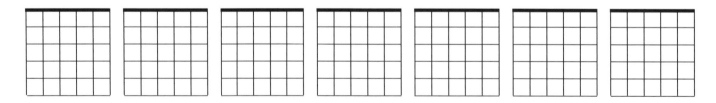

Song Set-Up & Chords

TUNING:　　　**CAPO:**　　　　**KEY:**

STRUM PATTERN:

PICK PATTERN:

Song Lyrics

INTRO

VERSE

CHORUS/HOOK

OUTRO

OTHER

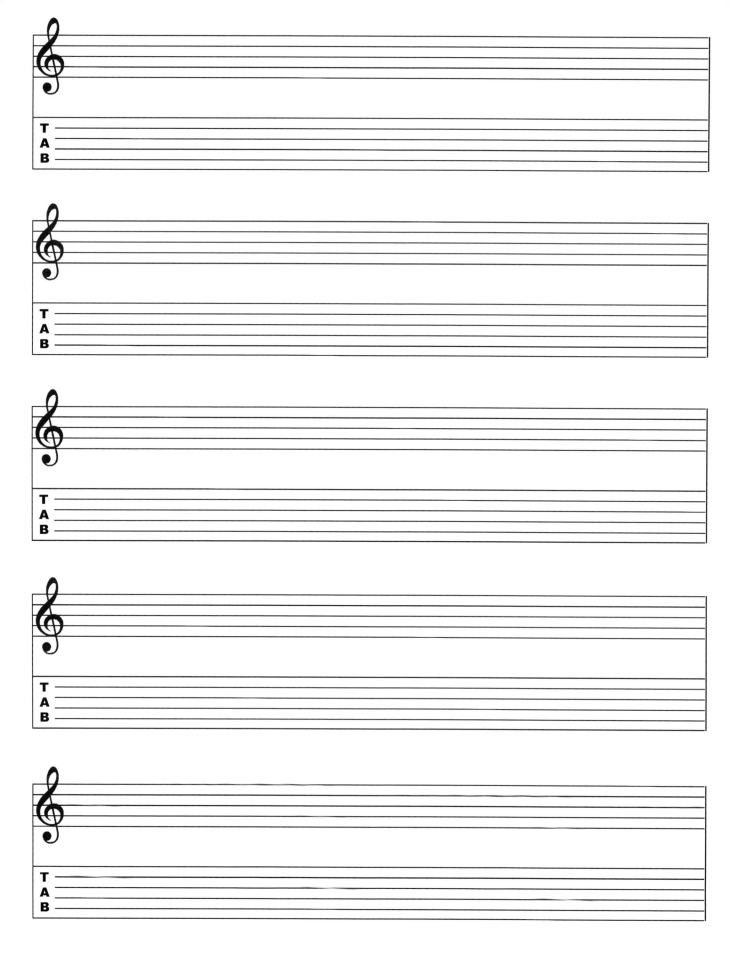

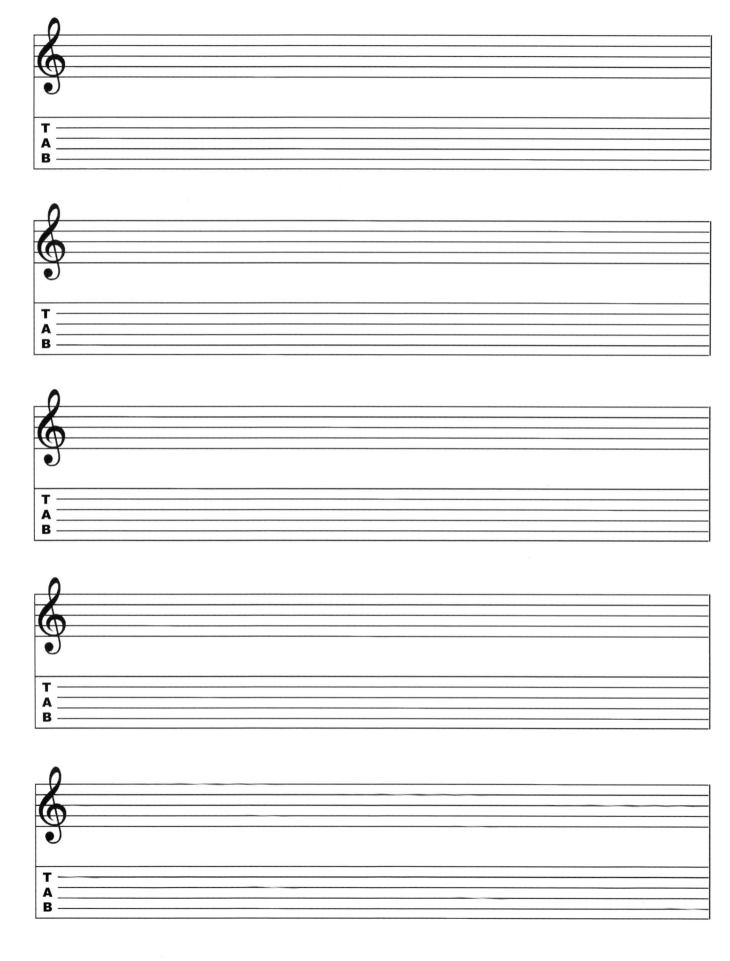

| 10 | **SONG** *Title* _____

Date Started: Date Completed:

SONG BRAINSTORMING NOTES (Jot down ideas for the song)

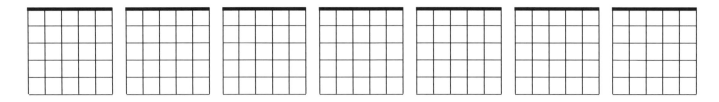

Song Set-Up & Chords

TUNING: **CAPO:**   **KEY:**

STRUM PATTERN:

PICK PATTERN:

Song Lyrics

INTRO

VERSE

CHORUS/HOOK

OUTRO

OTHER

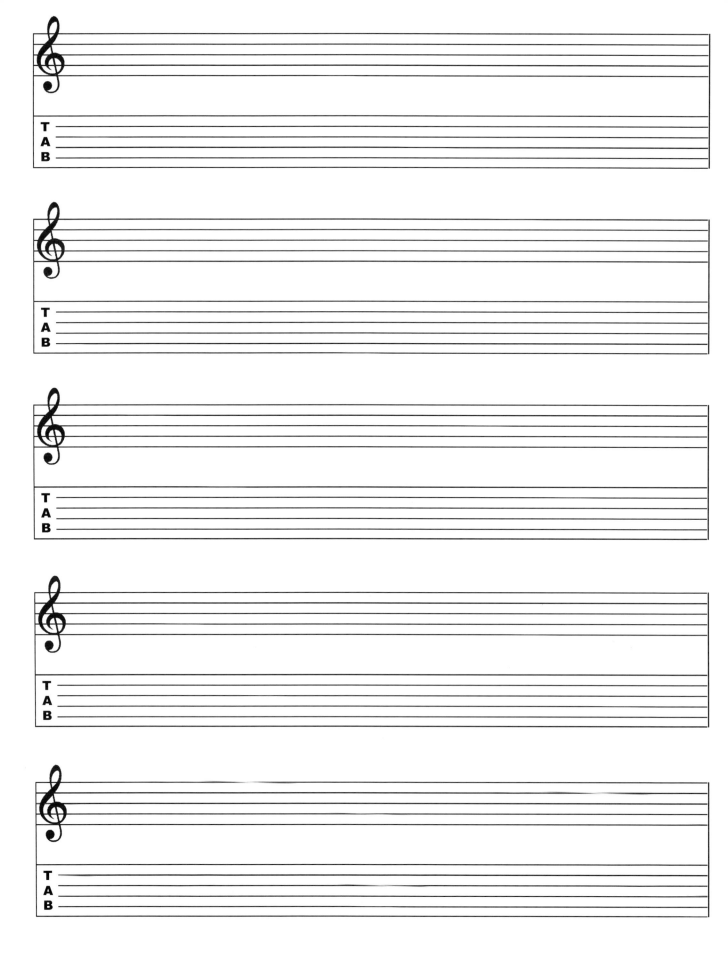

| 11 | **SONG** *Title* _____

Date Started: Date Completed:

SONG BRAINSTORMING NOTES (Jot down ideas for the song)

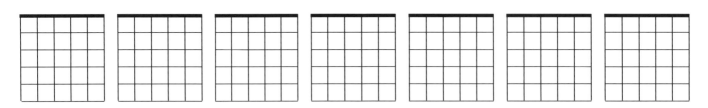

Song Set-Up & Chords

TUNING: **CAPO:**   **KEY:**

STRUM PATTERN:

PICK PATTERN:

Song Lyrics

INTRO

VERSE

CHORUS/HOOK

OUTRO

OTHER

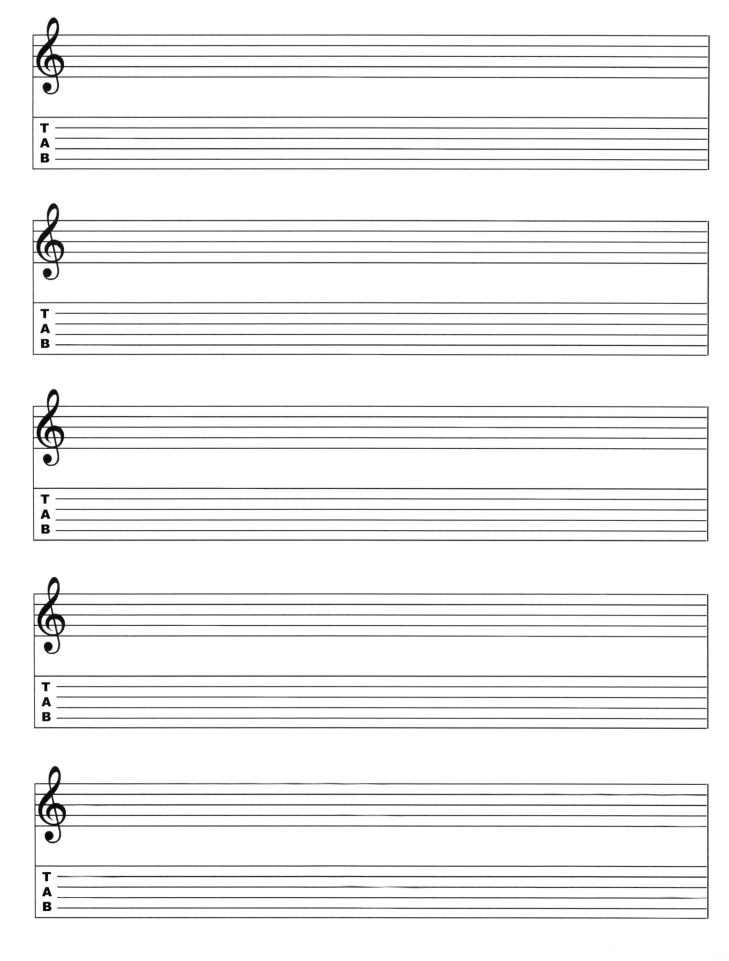

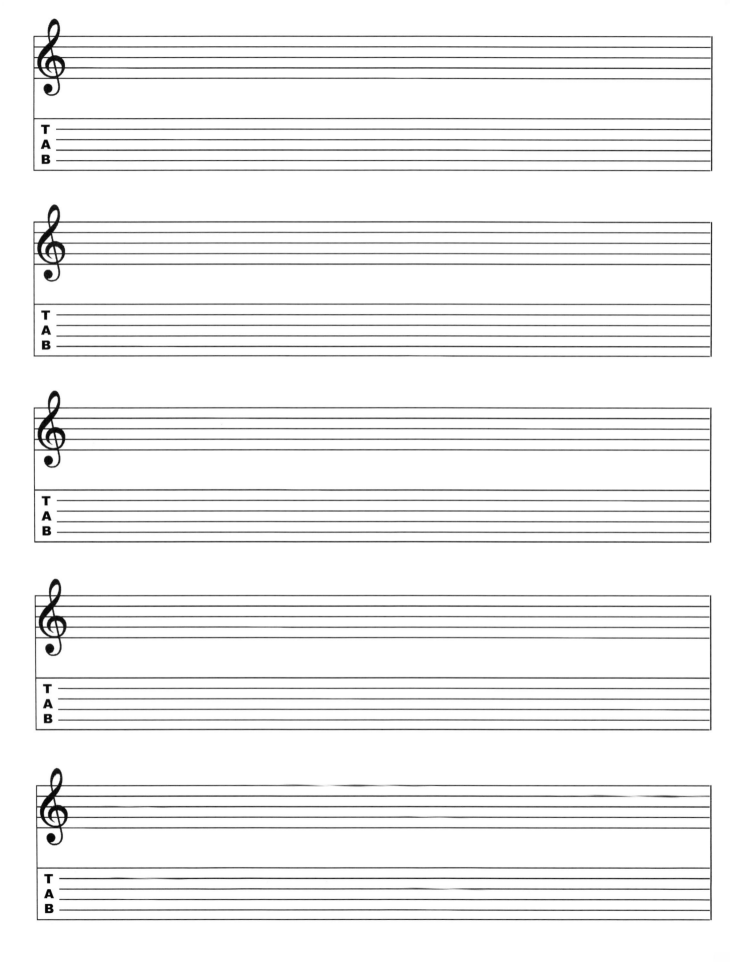

| 12 | **SONG** *Title* _____

Date Started: Date Completed:

SONG BRAINSTORMING NOTES (Jot down ideas for the song)

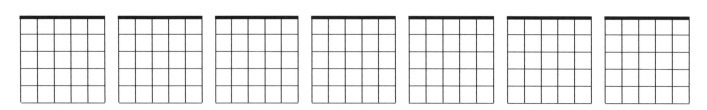

TUNING: **CAPO:**   **KEY:**

STRUM PATTERN:

PICK PATTERN:

Song Lyrics

INTRO

VERSE

CHORUS/HOOK

OUTRO

OTHER

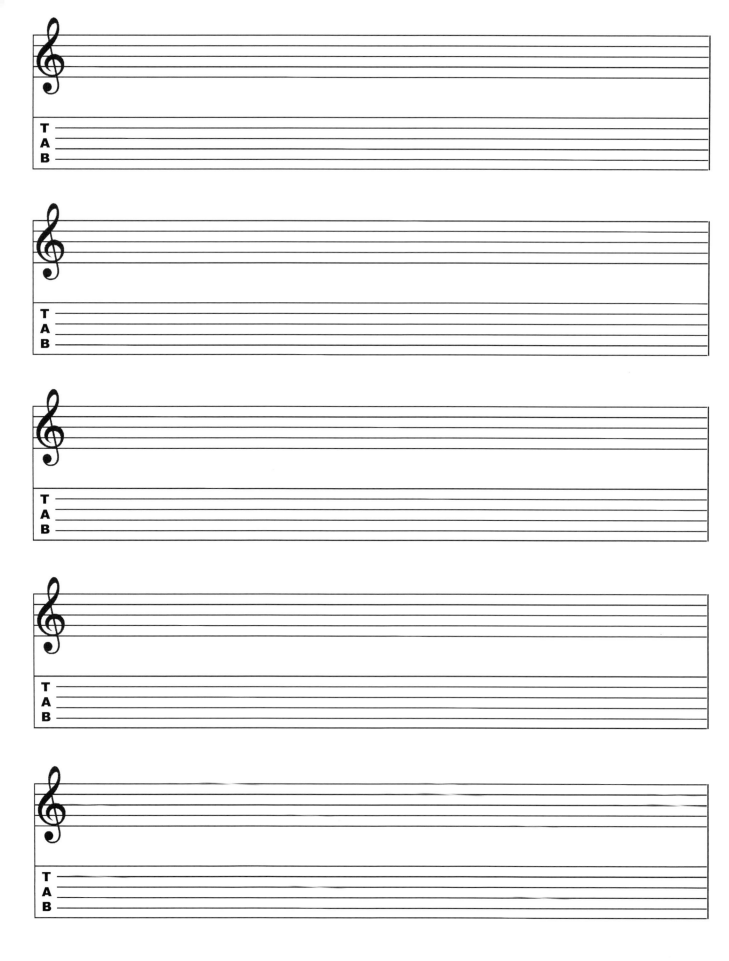

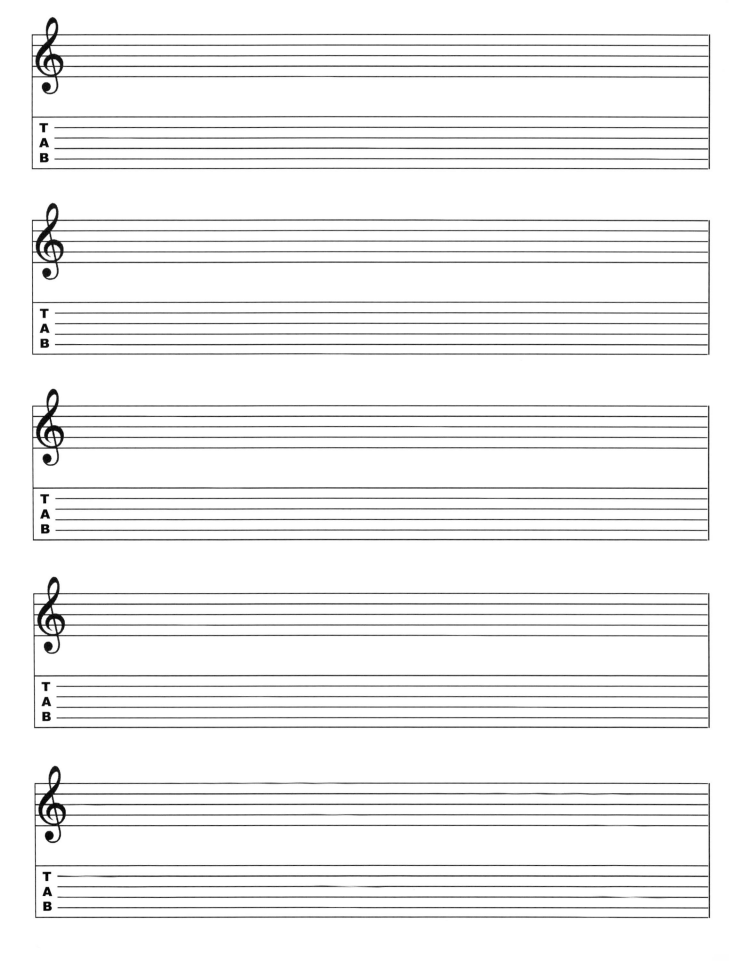

| 13 | **SONG** *Title* _____

Date Started: _____   Date Completed: _____

SONG BRAINSTORMING NOTES (Jot down ideas for the song)

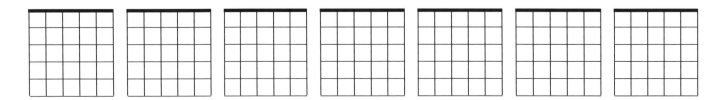

— *Song Set-Up & Chords* —

TUNING: **CAPO:**   **KEY:**

STRUM PATTERN:

PICK PATTERN:

Song Lyrics

INTRO

VERSE

CHORUS/HOOK

OUTRO

OTHER

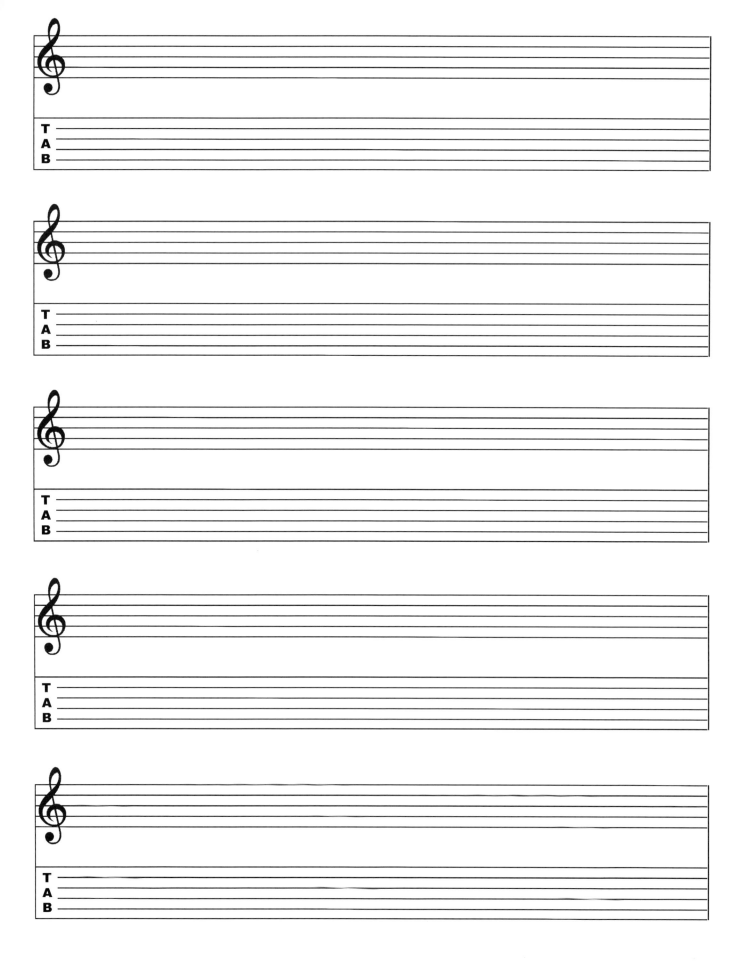

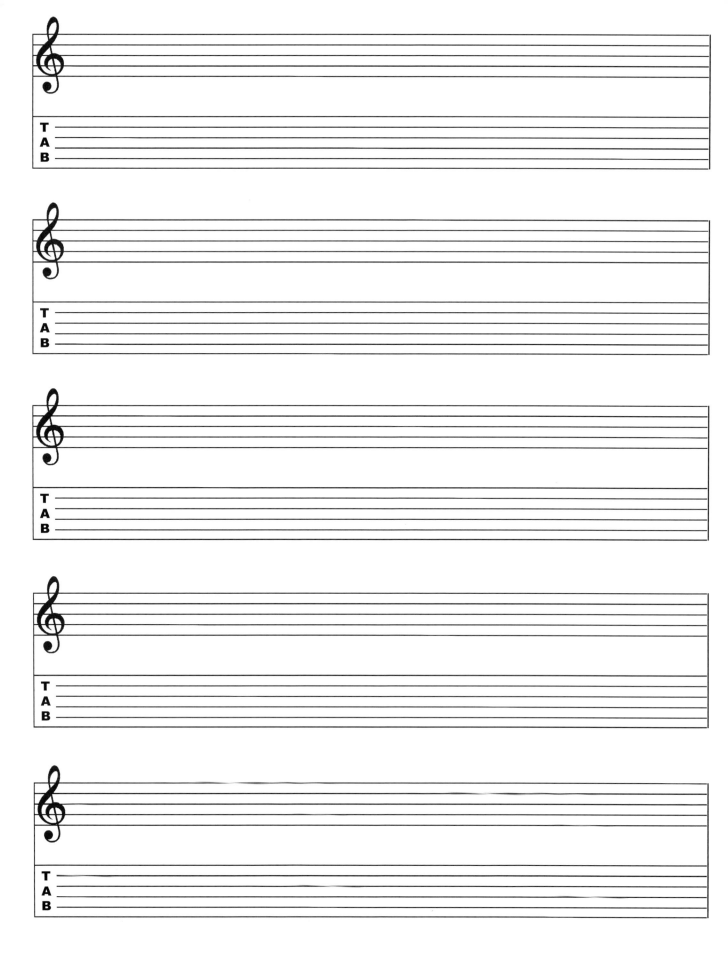

| 14 | **SONG** *Title* _____

Date Started: _____ Date Completed: _____

SONG BRAINSTORMING NOTES (Jot down ideas for the song)

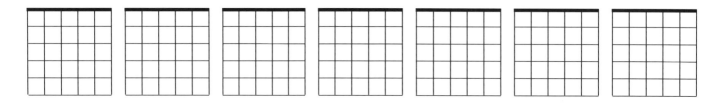

Song Set-Up & Chords

TUNING: **CAPO:**   **KEY:**

STRUM PATTERN:

PICK PATTERN:

Song Lyrics

INTRO

VERSE

CHORUS/HOOK

OUTRO

OTHER

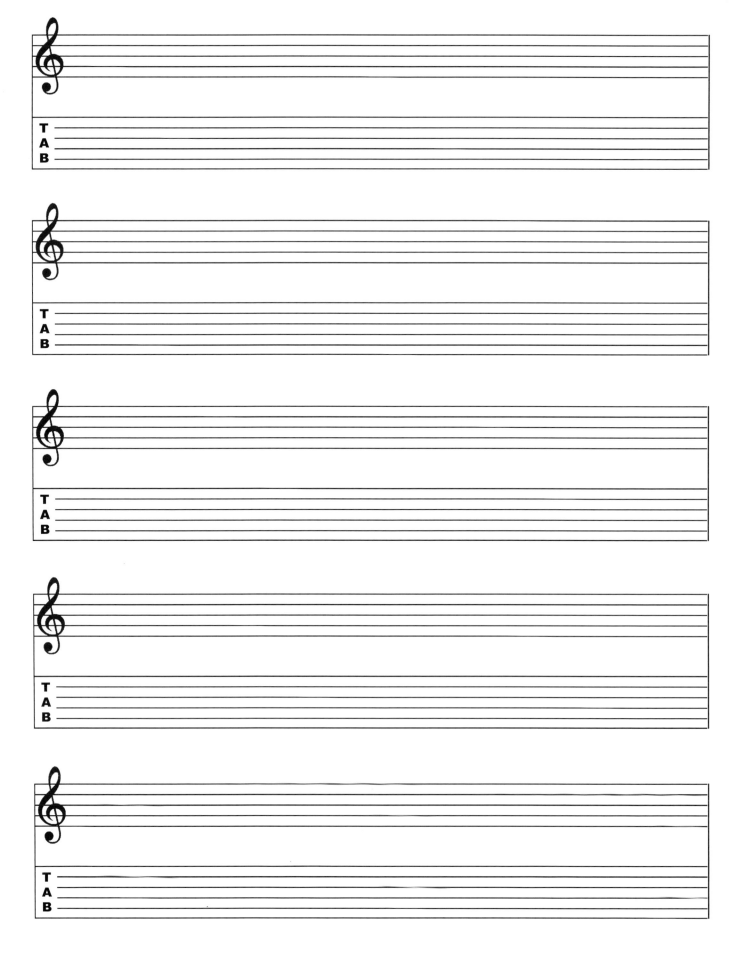

15 | **SONG** *Title* _____

Date Started: _____ Date Completed: _____

SONG BRAINSTORMING NOTES (Jot down ideas for the song)

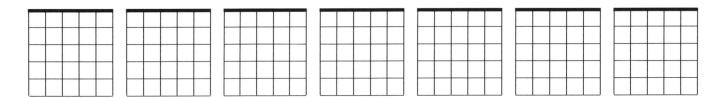

Song Set-Up & Chords

TUNING:　　　**CAPO:**　　　**KEY:**

STRUM PATTERN:

PICK PATTERN:

Song Lyrics

INTRO

VERSE

CHORUS/HOOK

OUTRO

OTHER

| 16 | **SONG** *Title* _____

Date Started: Date Completed:

SONG BRAINSTORMING NOTES (Jot down ideas for the song)

Song Set-Up & Chords

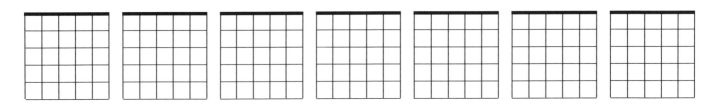

TUNING: **CAPO:**   **KEY:**

STRUM PATTERN:

PICK PATTERN:

Song Lyrics

INTRO

VERSE

CHORUS/HOOK

OUTRO

OTHER

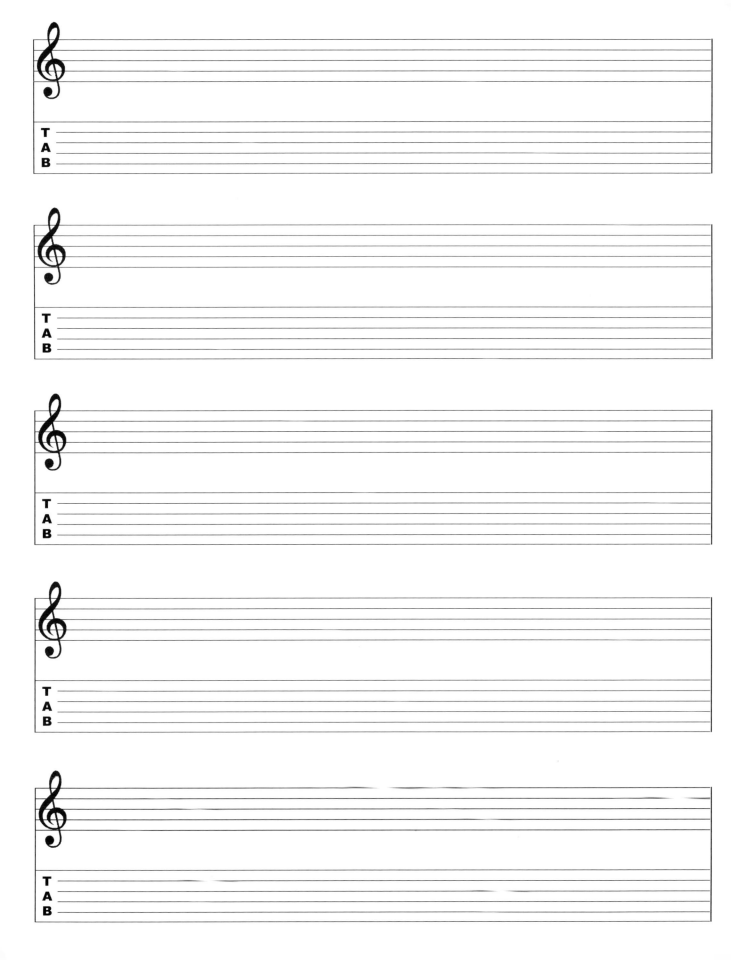

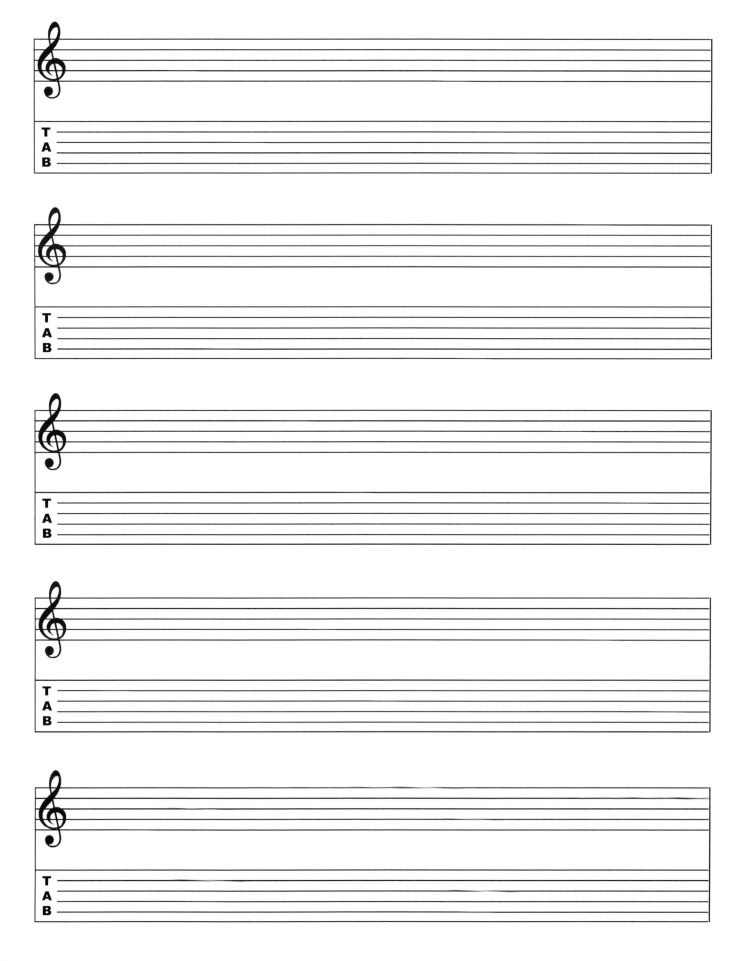

| 17 | **SONG** *Title* _____

Date Started: Date Completed:

SONG BRAINSTORMING NOTES (Jot down ideas for the song)

Song Set-Up & Chords

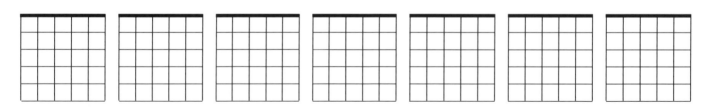

TUNING: **CAPO:**   **KEY:**

STRUM PATTERN:

PICK PATTERN:

Song Lyrics

INTRO

VERSE

CHORUS/HOOK

OUTRO

OTHER

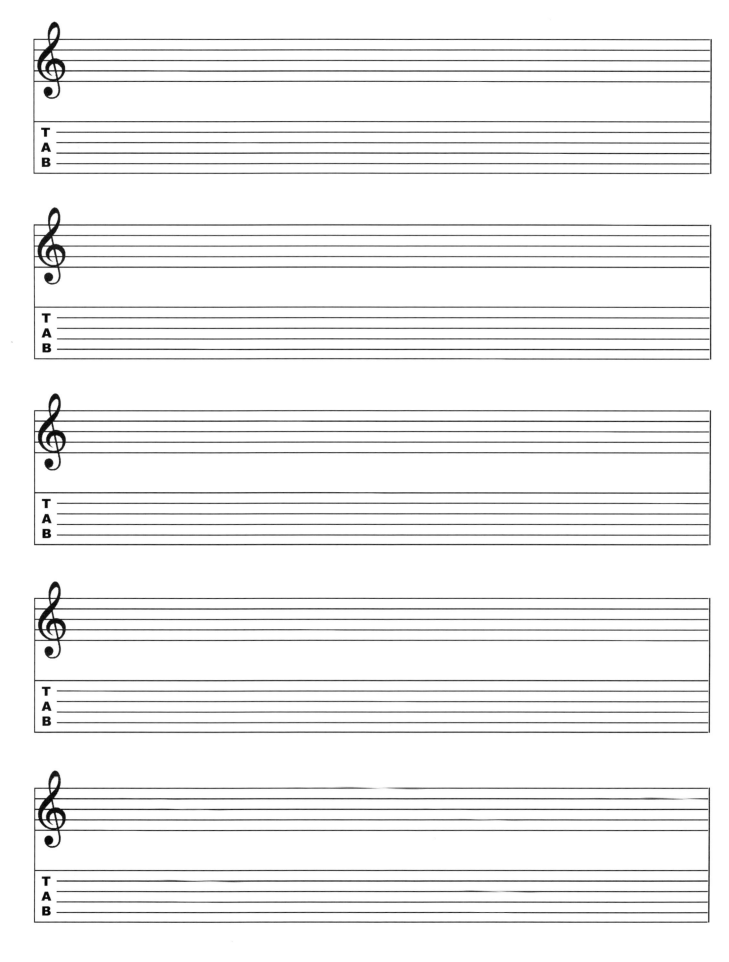

| 18 | **SONG** *Title* _____

Date Started: Date Completed:

SONG BRAINSTORMING NOTES (Jot down ideas for the song)

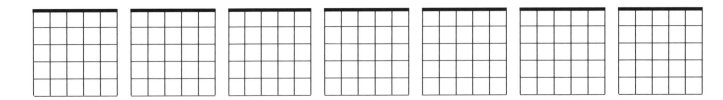

Song Set-Up & Chords

TUNING: **CAPO:**   **KEY:**

STRUM PATTERN:

PICK PATTERN:

Song Lyrics

INTRO

VERSE

CHORUS/HOOK

OUTRO

OTHER

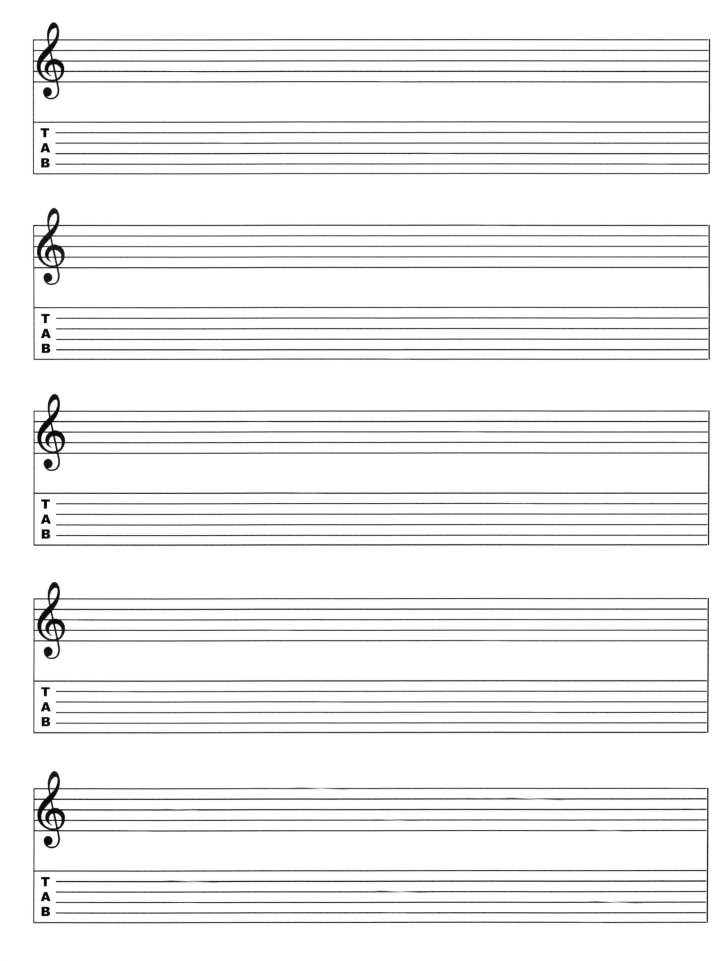

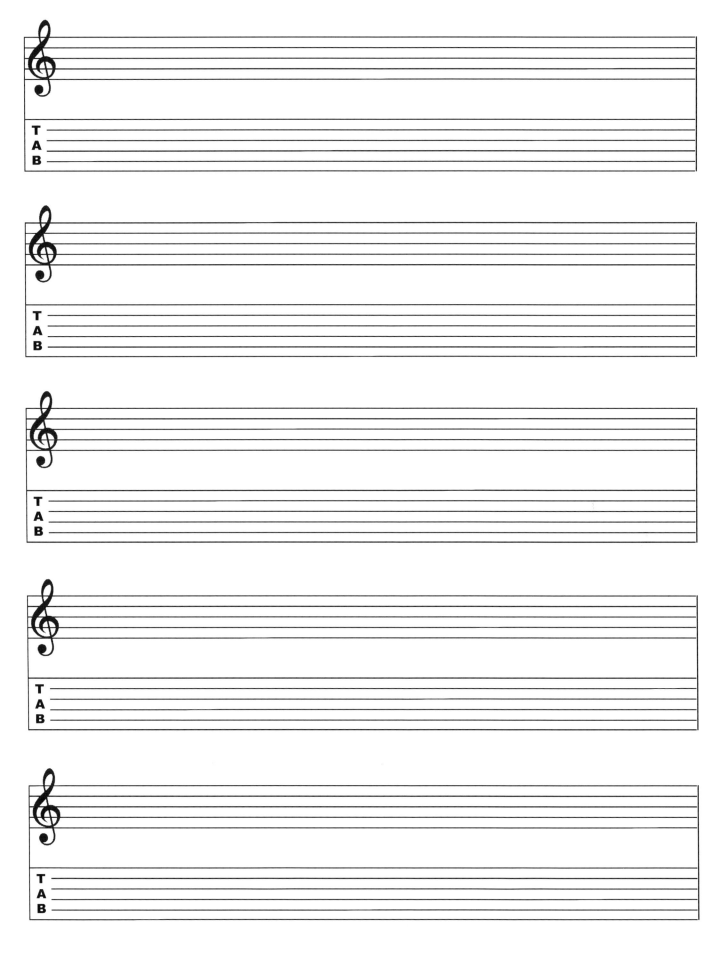

19 | SONG *Title* _____

Date Started: Date Completed:

SONG BRAINSTORMING NOTES (Jot down ideas for the song)

Song Set-Up & Chords

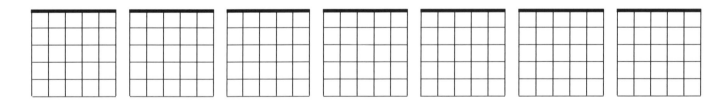

TUNING:　　　**CAPO:**　　　**KEY:**

STRUM PATTERN:

PICK PATTERN:

Song Lyrics

INTRO

VERSE

CHORUS/HOOK

OUTRO

OTHER

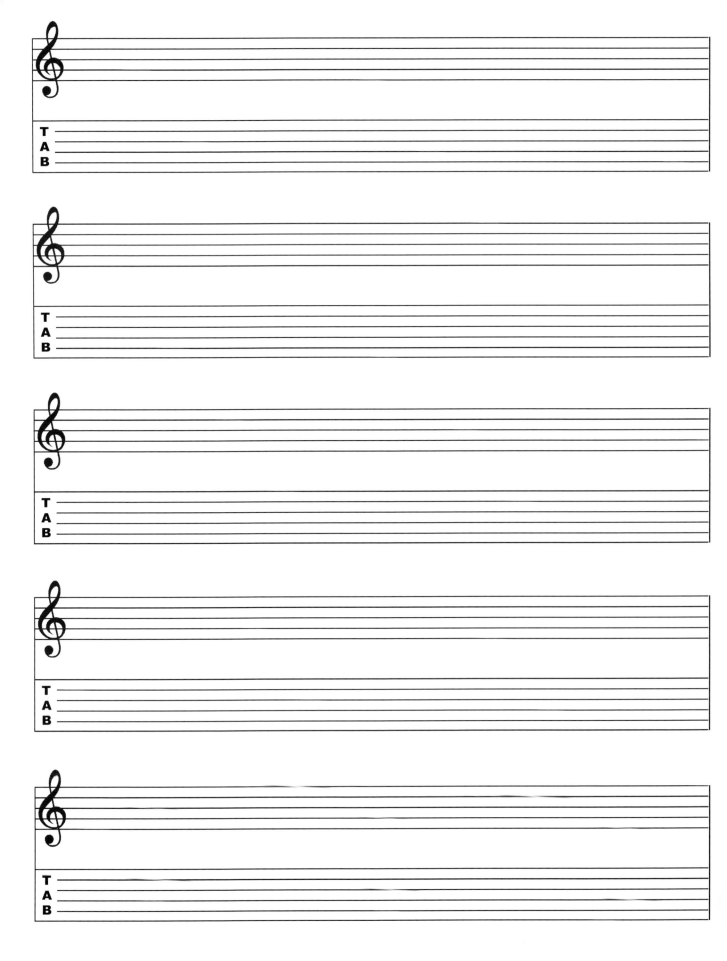

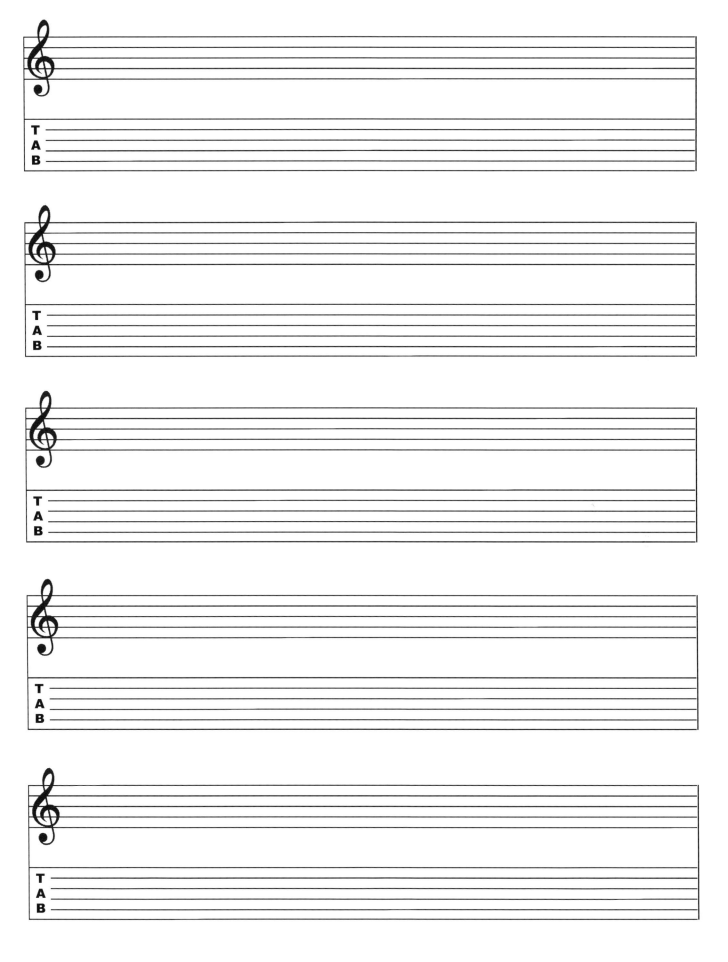

| 20 | **SONG** *Title* _____

Date Started: Date Completed:

SONG BRAINSTORMING NOTES (Jot down ideas for the song)

―――――――― *Song Set-Up & Chords* ――――――――

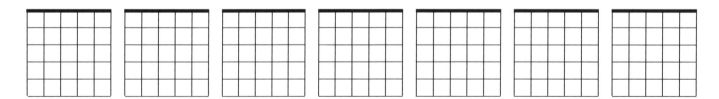

TUNING: **CAPO:**   **KEY:**

STRUM PATTERN:

PICK PATTERN:

Song Lyrics

INTRO

VERSE

CHORUS/HOOK

OUTRO

OTHER

21 SONG *Title* _____

Date Started: Date Completed:

SONG BRAINSTORMING NOTES (Jot down ideas for the song)

Song Set-Up & Chords

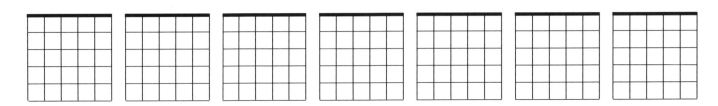

TUNING: **CAPO:**   **KEY:**

STRUM PATTERN:

PICK PATTERN:

Song Lyrics

INTRO

VERSE

CHORUS/HOOK

OUTRO

OTHER

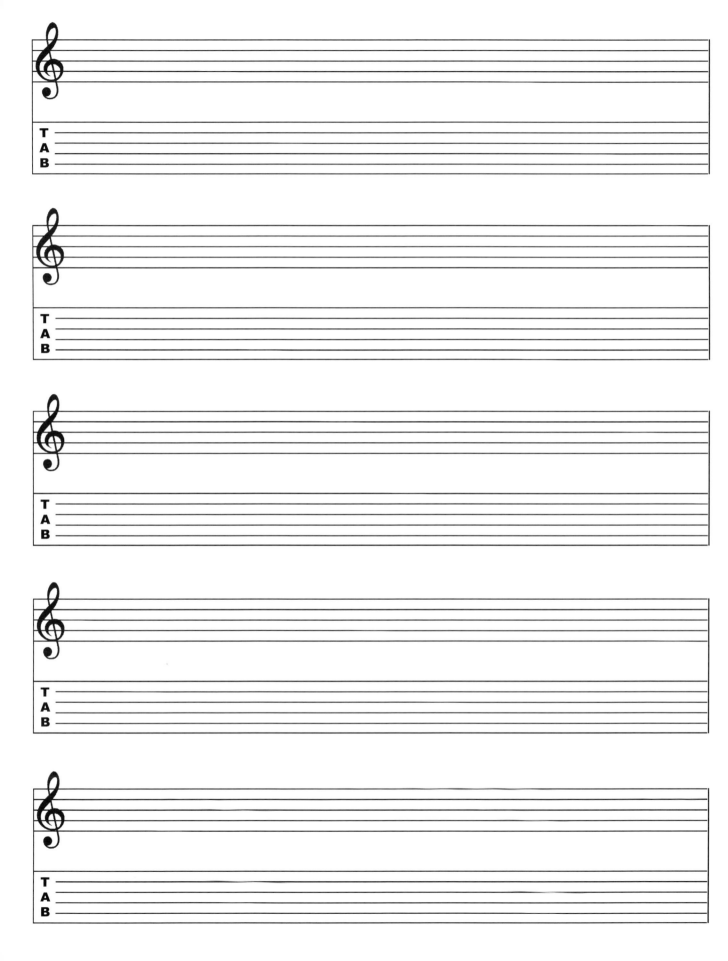

| 22 | **SONG** *Title* _____

Date Started: Date Completed:

SONG BRAINSTORMING NOTES (Jot down ideas for the song)

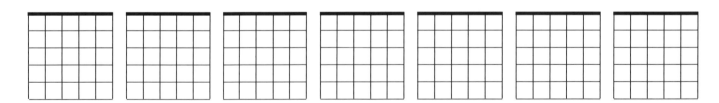

Song Set-Up & Chords

TUNING:　　　　**CAPO:**　　　　　　**KEY:**

STRUM PATTERN:

PICK PATTERN:

Song Lyrics

INTRO

VERSE

CHORUS/HOOK

OUTRO

OTHER

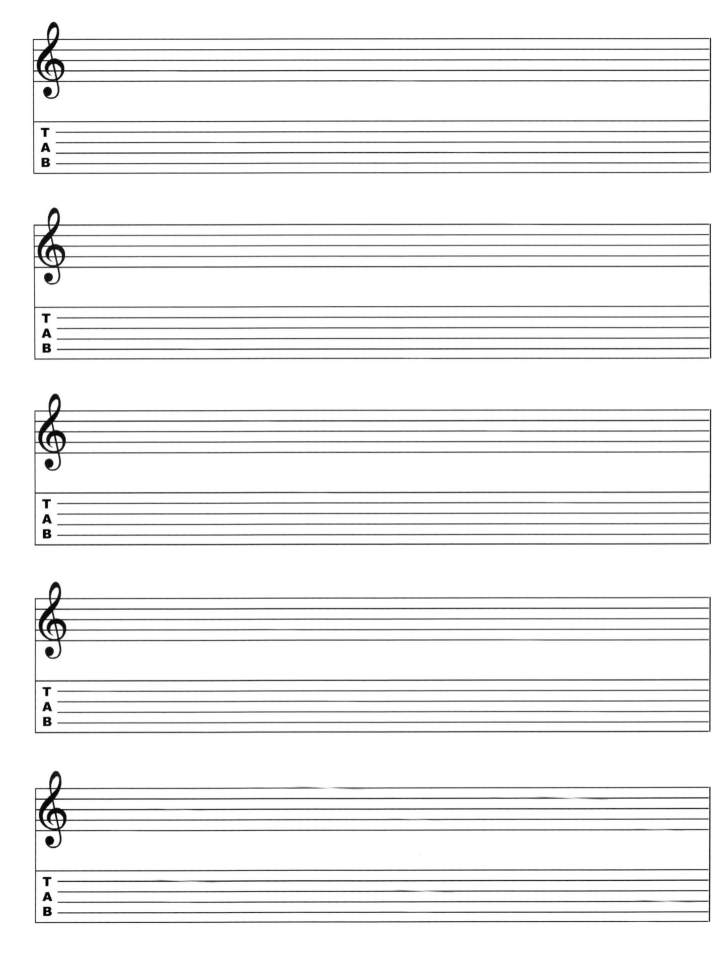

| 23 | **SONG** *Title* _____

Date Started: _____ Date Completed: _____

SONG BRAINSTORMING NOTES (Jot down ideas for the song)

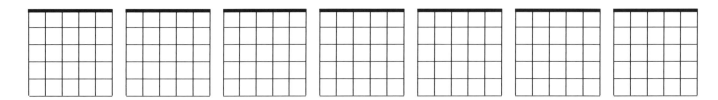

— *Song Set-Up & Chords* —

TUNING: **CAPO:**   **KEY:**

STRUM PATTERN:

PICK PATTERN:

Song Lyrics

INTRO

VERSE

CHORUS/HOOK

OUTRO

OTHER

| 24 | **SONG** *Title* _____

Date Started: _____ Date Completed: _____

SONG BRAINSTORMING NOTES (Jot down ideas for the song)

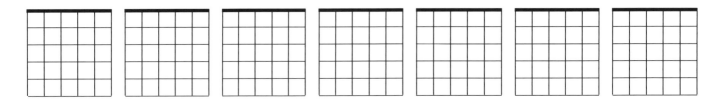

Song Set-Up & Chords

TUNING: **CAPO:**   **KEY:**

STRUM PATTERN:

PICK PATTERN:

Song Lyrics

INTRO

VERSE

CHORUS/HOOK

OUTRO

OTHER

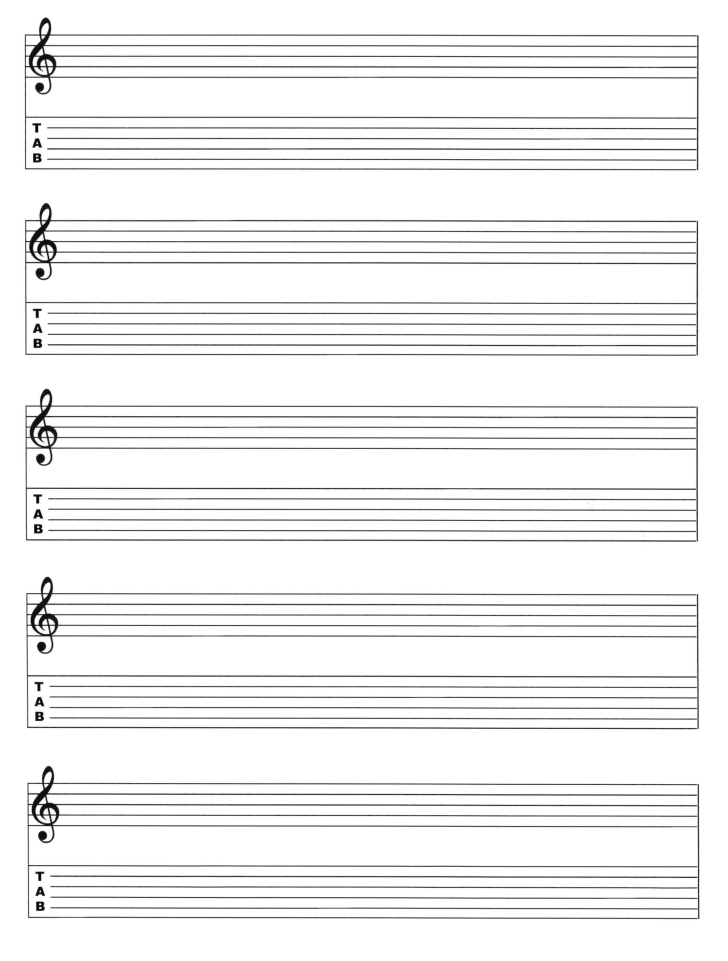

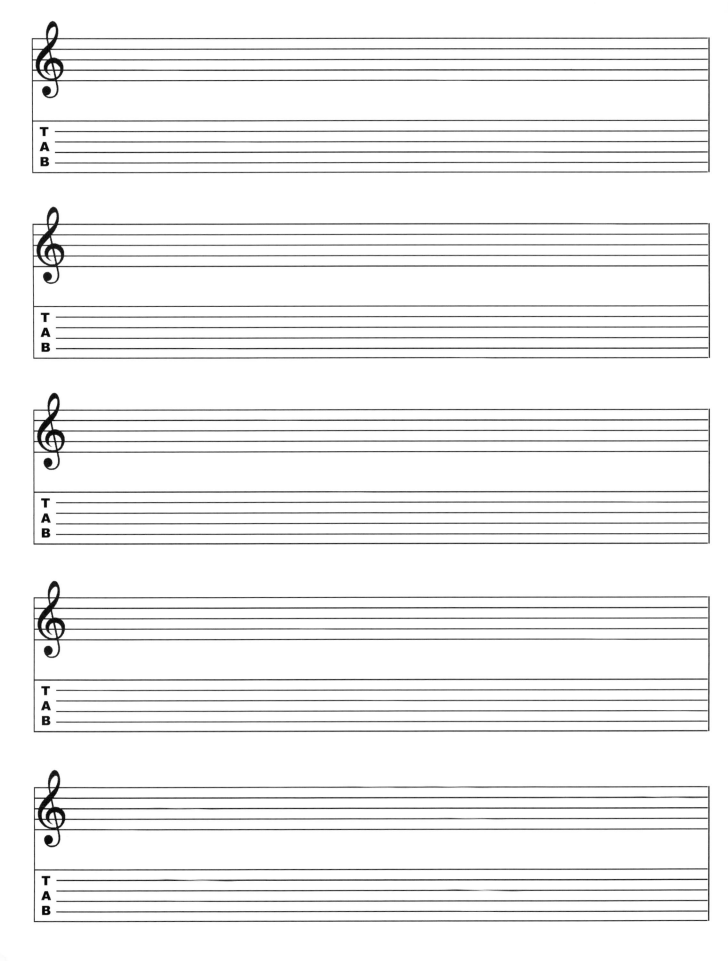

| 25 | **SONG** *Title* _____ |

Date Started: Date Completed:

SONG BRAINSTORMING NOTES (Jot down ideas for the song)

Song Set-Up & Chords

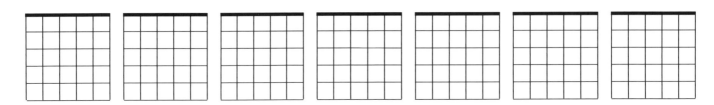

TUNING: **CAPO:**   **KEY:**

STRUM PATTERN:

PICK PATTERN:

Song Lyrics

INTRO

VERSE

CHORUS/HOOK

OUTRO

OTHER

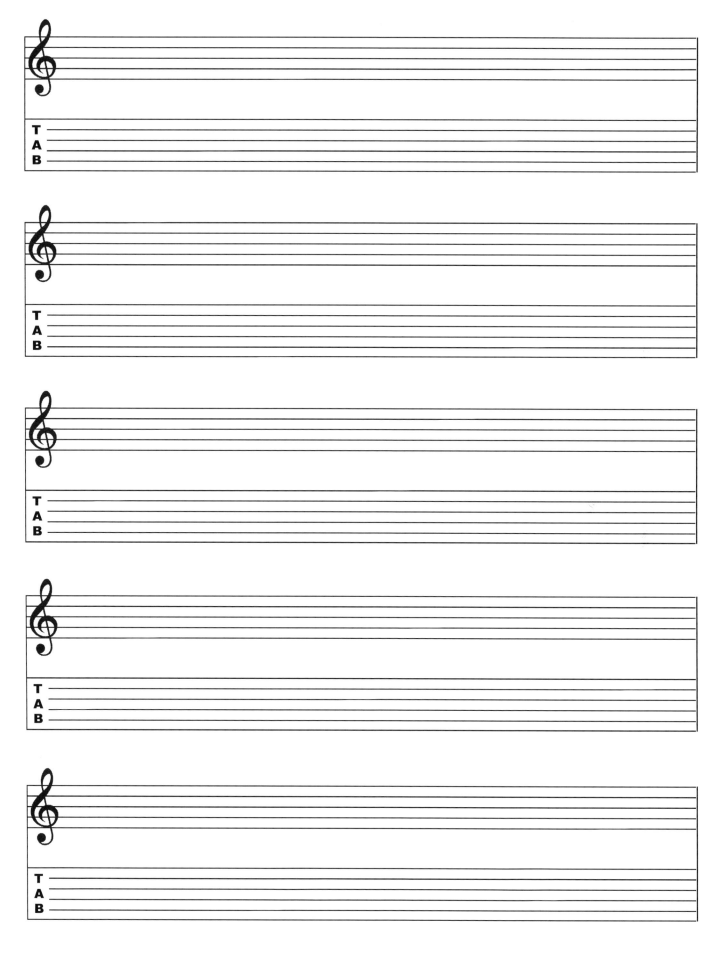

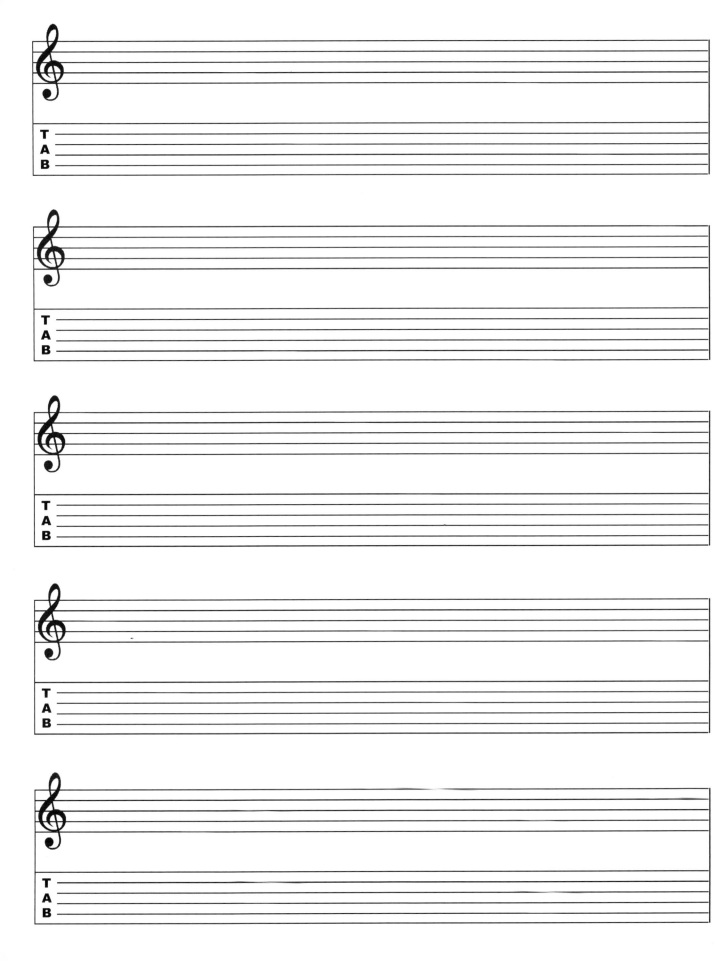

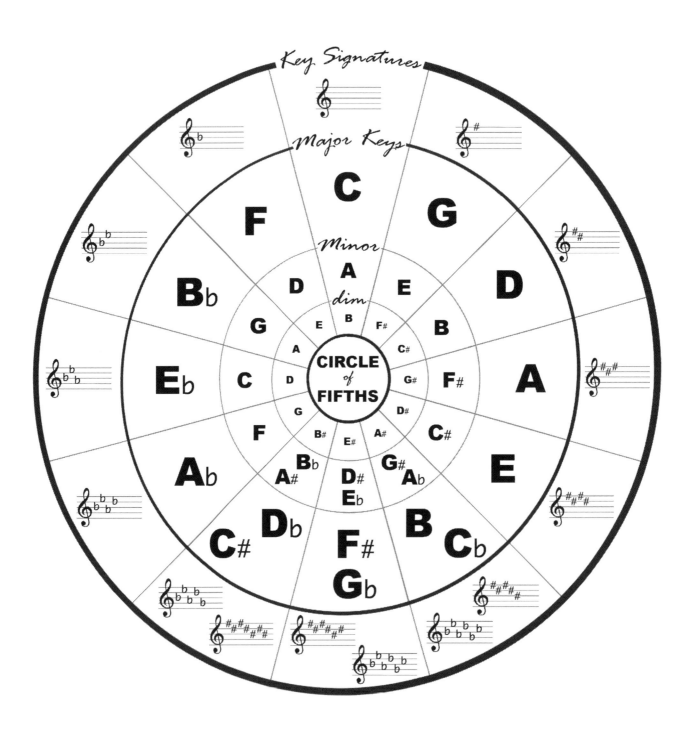

Song Writing References

BASIC Tips

TIPS & BASIC STRUCTURE OF SONGS

STEP 1: Brainstorm ideas, themes, inspirations, metaphors, stories
- *this is where you should come up with some hook/chorus ideas*
- *choose topics you are passionate about and that you know*
- *most songs often tell a story about loss, heartbreak, betrayal, family etc.*
- *tell a full story (make sure your song has a beginning, middle and end)*
- *jot down key words that describe your topic (create descriptive imagery)*
- *make a list of words that rhyme with your main key words (rhyme clusters)*
- *avoid using words just because they rhyme*
- *remember not all your lines have to rhyme*
- *look to poems and your favorite country artists for inspiration*

STEP 2: Choose a couple of beats to experiment with for feel and speed
- *find free beats online, from existing soundtracks or create your own*
- *metronomes help to keep track of the beat with your guitar strumming*
- *most songs are usually written in major keys (G, A, C, D, E, and F)*
- *common chord progression (1st chord in the key's scale, 4th, 5th, 1st)*
- *songs normally have 4 beats per bar/line with chord changes every 4-8 beats*
- *songs normally have 8 bars/lines per chorus/hook*
- *songs normally have 16 bars/lines per verse*

STEP 3: Write some lyrics and match them to your beat
- *divide your words into syllables to make it easier to match your beat*
- *avoid telling how you feel BUT show how you feel through the storytelling*
- *create some rhyming schemes for your verses (how the song will rhyme)*
- *set up a song structure for your song (you can really do what you want)*

   Some examples:
   1. Verse-Chorus-Verse-Chorus-Verse-Chorus (Intro & Outro omitted)
   2. Intro-Chorus-Verse-Chorus-Verse-Chorus-Outro
   3. Intro-Verse-Chorus-Verse-Chorus-Verse-Chorus-Outro
   4. Intro-Hook-Verse-Hook-Bridge-Verse-Chorus-Outro

STEP 4: Practice your song over and over and make edits if it's needed
- *when practicing, listen for what is working or not working*
- *make any changes to help the flow of your lyrics*
- *add emotion to your song so people can feel it through your words*
- *practice projecting your voice while you sing and adding other instruments*

STEP 5: Now perform it, record it and share it with the world!
- *this is your masterpiece - so take pride in it but also be open to critique, comments and suggestions from your audience*
- *the only way to get better at writing and performing your songs is so keep writing and performing*
- *the most important thing is to enjoy the process!*

GETTING *Started*

COMMON SONG STRUCTURE (Experiment and get creative with your own song structures)

INTRO

	Beat 1	Beat 2	Beat 3	Beat 4
Bar 1				
Bar 2				
Bar 3				
Bar 4				
Bar 5				
Bar 6				
Bar 7				
Bar 8				

Normally 4 Beats per Bar/Line and up to 8 Bars
(not always included)

Can be speech, sound effects or other noises

**1 Bar = 1 Line of Song
4 Bars = 1 Quatrain**

VERSE

Bar 1				
Bar 2				
Bar 3				
Bar 4				
Bar 5				
Bar 6				
Bar 7				
Bar 8				
Bar 9				
Bar 10				
Bar 11				
Bar 12				
Bar 13				
Bar 14				
Bar 15				
Bar 16				

Usually repeated 3 times during the song

16 Bars per Verse

Can be 8, 12, 16 or 24 bars - most songs have 16 bars

*This is where you sing about the topic
- make the points to support your overall theme*

CHORUS/HOOK

Bar 1				
Bar 2				
Bar 3				
Bar 4				
Bar 5				
Bar 6				
Bar 7				
Bar 8				

Usually repeated 3 to 4 times during the song

Normally it's 1 quatrain repeated twice to make 8 bars total

This is where the main idea and meaning of your song is described to peek the audience's attention

VERSE>>CHORUS >>VERSE>>CHORUS>>VERSE>>CHORUS
Repeat the chorus and verse as many times as you like

AFTER/BEFORE CHORUS and/or BRIDGE
*- Not necessary but you can add a few lines of song before or after your chorus to assist it or a bridge between two choruses
(add the bridge near the end of the song to add more interest to the lyrics)*

OUTRO

Bar 1				
Bar 2				
Bar 3				
Bar 4				
Bar 5				
Bar 6				
Bar 7				
Bar 8				

Up to 8 Bars
(not always included)

Can be anything to lower the energy level and end off the song

BASIC *Schemes*

RHYMING SCHEME PATTERNS

TYPE OF RHYMES:

End Rhymes – The last word of the line rhymes.
Internal Rhymes – Two words in the same line rhymes.
Slant or Near Rhymes – The vowel or consonant sounds of two words in the same line rhymes (the sound of the words are similar but do not actually rhyme).
Identical Rhymes – When the same word is used again.

X = Line does not RHYME   **)** *= Lines RHYME*

RHYMING RESOURCES & REFERENCES

Rhyming & Helpful Websites:

- www.b-rhymes.com
- www.colemizestudios.com
- www.dillfrog.com
- www.double-rhyme.com
- www.genius.com
- www.rapmetrics.com
- www.rapscript.net
- www.rhymebrain.com
- www.rhymebuster.com
- www.rhymedb.com
- www.rhymer.com
- www.rhymezone.com

Other Resources:

- www.ascap.com
- www.audiosauna.com
- www.bmi.com
- www.chordchord.com
- www.countryhound.com
- www.fachords.com
- www.handmetheaux.com
- www.lyricsfreak.com
- www.metronomer.com
- www.musicindustryhowto.com
- www.mysongcoach.com
- www.reverbnation.com
- www.robinfrederick.com
- www.song-lyrics-generator.org.uk
- www.songwriteruniverse.com
- www.writeexpress.com
- www.writerbot.com

My Favorite Resources:

1. _____
2. _____
3. _____
4. _____
5. _____
6. _____
7. _____
8. _____
9. _____
10. _____
11. _____
12. _____
13. _____
14. _____
15. _____
16. _____
17. _____
18. _____
19. _____
20. _____
21. _____
22. _____
23. _____
24. _____
25. _____

BASIC *Chords*

COMMONLY USED CHORDS (Add your own favorite to the list)

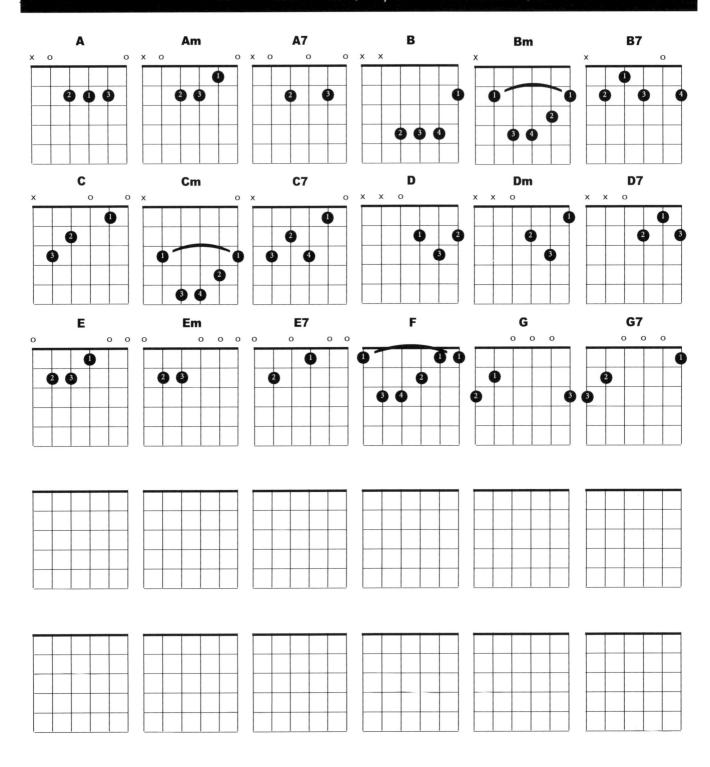

* These are the most common chords used in songs - learning them will benefit you!
* Add to this list with your own favorite chords

GETTING Started

COMMONLY USED CHORD PROGRESSIONS (Add your own favorite to the list)

Common Chord Progressions - *chord progressions in music are often very simple with few or no augmented or diminished chords in them at all. Some great Country music of all time only use 3 chords!*

My Favorite Progressions:

1. _____
2. _____
3. _____
4. _____
5. _____
6. _____
7. _____
8. _____
9. _____
10. _____
11. _____
12. _____
13. _____
14. _____
15. _____
16. _____
17. _____
18. _____
19. _____
20. _____
21. _____
22. _____
23. _____
24. _____
25. _____

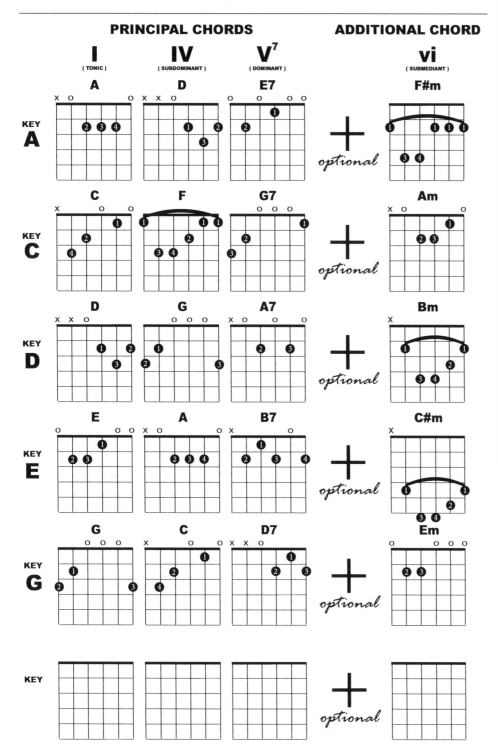

TITLES Collection

✓	TITLE IDEAS (When you think of good titles record them here so you can use them for future songs)

GETTING *Ideas*

GENRE/TYPE OF SONG	WHERE I USED IT	Notes

TITLES *Collection*

✓	TITLE IDEAS (When you think of good titles record them here so you can use them for future songs)

GETTING *Ideas*

GENRE/TYPE OF SONG	WHERE I USED IT	Notes

HOOKS Collection

✓	HOOK IDEAS (Guitar Licks, Melody Lines, Lyrics etc. that you can use in future songs)

GETTING *Ideas*

GENRE/TYPE OF SONG	WHERE I USED IT	Notes

HOOKS *Collection*

✓	HOOK IDEAS (Guitar Licks, Melody Lines, Lyrics etc. that you can use in future songs)

GETTING *Ideas*

GENRE/TYPE OF SONG	WHERE I USED IT	Notes

Notes

Printed in Great Britain
by Amazon